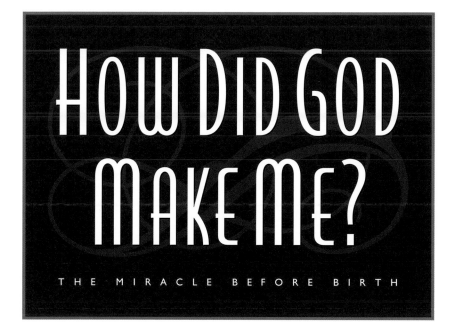

How Did God Make Me?

THE MIRACLE BEFORE BIRTH

MATT & LISA JACOBSON

ILLUSTRATIONS BY LINDA WELLER AND DAVID DANZ
SELECTED PHOTOS BY LENNART NILSSON

Gold 'n' Honey BOOKS

TO
BRITAIN MATTHEW MORE JACOBSON,
SAVOURY MICHELLE LORENE JACOBSON,
AND
VIENNA LISÉ PATRICIA JACOBSON

May you know, love, and defend the truth.

HOW DID GOD MAKE ME?

published by Gold'n'Honey Books
a part of the Questar publishing family

©1996 by Matthew and Lisa Jacobson
Illustrations ©1996 by Linda Weller and ©1996 by David Danz
Selected photography by Lennart Nilsson (from *A Child Is Born,* Dell Publishing Co.)
Photos also by Tony Stone Images and Photo Researchers, Inc.

Design by David Uttley

International Standard Book Number: 0-88070-914-6

Printed in the United States of America

For information:
Questar Publishers, Inc. • Post Office Box 1720 • Sisters, Oregon 97759

97 98 99 00 01 02 03 — 10 9 8 7 6 5 4 3 2

...Trailing clouds of glory do we come
from God who is our home.
Heaven lies about us in our infancy!

WILLIAM WORDSWORTH

Mommy, *baby Jessica sure is small.*

Yes, she is. But you're getting so big!
Have you finished your lunch, my big boy?

Just a few peas left.

Good. When you're finished,
we can read a book together.

Mommy, was I ever as small as Jessica?

Yes. A lot smaller, in fact.

Was I this small?

Even smaller.

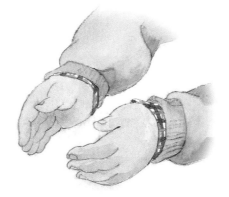

W*as I this small?*

Smaller than that.
You were even smaller than a pea.

That is small! Did you love me when I was so small?

Oh, yes. Daddy and I loved you.
God made you special right from the start.

13

Mommy, *how did God make me?*

That's a good question.
And the answer makes a wonderful story.

Daddy and I were so excited the day you were born.
But that wasn't the beginning.
Many months earlier, God created you from two special parts—
one from Mommy and one from Daddy.
Those two parts came together to make up the tiny, tiny you.
You were only the size of a little dot.
Can you believe it?

THE BEGINNING

After a part from the mother and a part from the father come together to begin a baby's life, the baby is about this size:

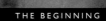

ONE WEEK OLD

THREE WEEKS OLD

FIVE WEEKS OLD

Was that when I was in your tummy?

Yes. There's a special place inside mommies that's just for babies. It's called a uterus.

Did I like it in there?

Oh, yes. It's the perfect place for a baby.

But how could I be alive?

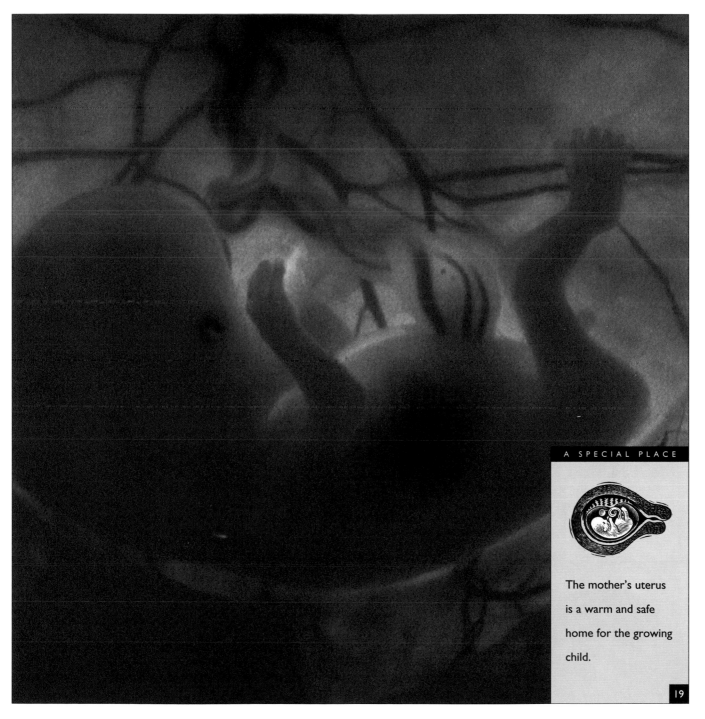

A SPECIAL PLACE

The mother's uterus
is a warm and safe
home for the growing
child.

19

Let me show you. Hug me tight, and listen close.
What do you hear?

Your heart. Thump, thump, thump!

That's it. And *your* heart started beating only three weeks
after God first made you—
when you were as small as that tiny dot.

20

SIX WEEKS OLD

Can you find the baby's heart? It is red, and already pumping at about 150 beats every minute.

21

Then *what happened?*

Well, you kept on growing.
After you lived inside Mommy only eight weeks,
you already had every part of your body
that you have right now.
But you still had lots more growing to do.

22

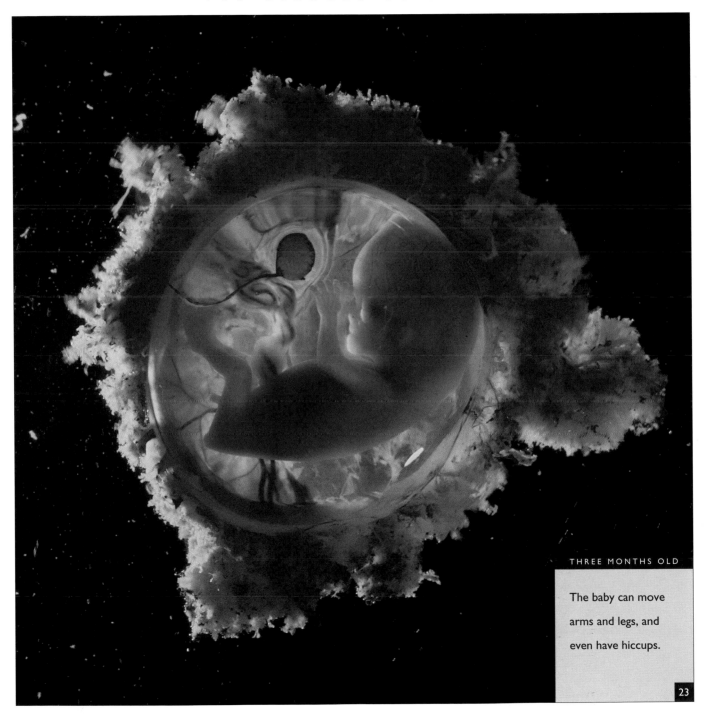

THREE MONTHS OLD

The baby can move
arms and legs, and
even have hiccups.

23

Did I have my nose?

Oh, yes. You had a cute little button nose.
You also had beautiful eyes.

THIRTEEN WEEKS OLD

Behind closed eyelids, the baby's eyes soon begin to see dim light coming from outside the mother's body.

25

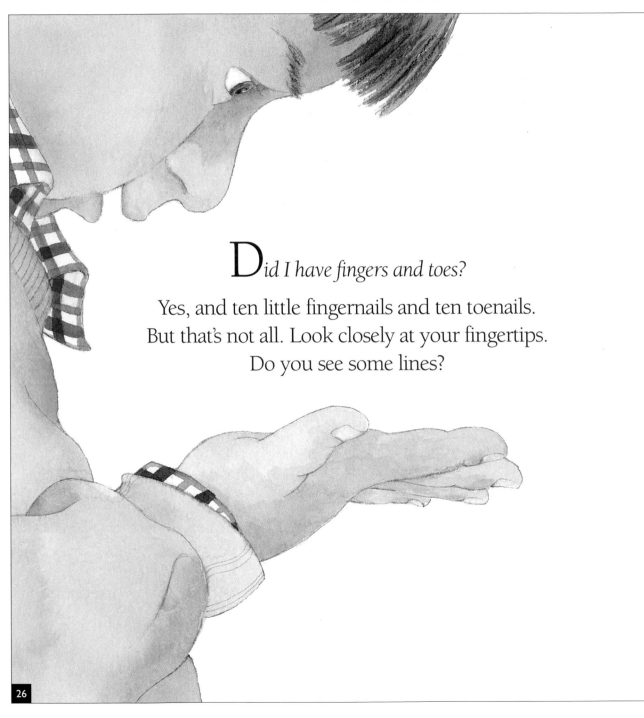

Did *I have fingers and toes?*

Yes, and ten little fingernails and ten toenails.
But that's not all. Look closely at your fingertips.
Do you see some lines?

T*hose little swirly lines?*

Right. Those are your special fingerprints.
No one else in the whole world has
fingerprints just like yours.
You are the only person in the world just like you!

Wow, Mommy, I really like this story.

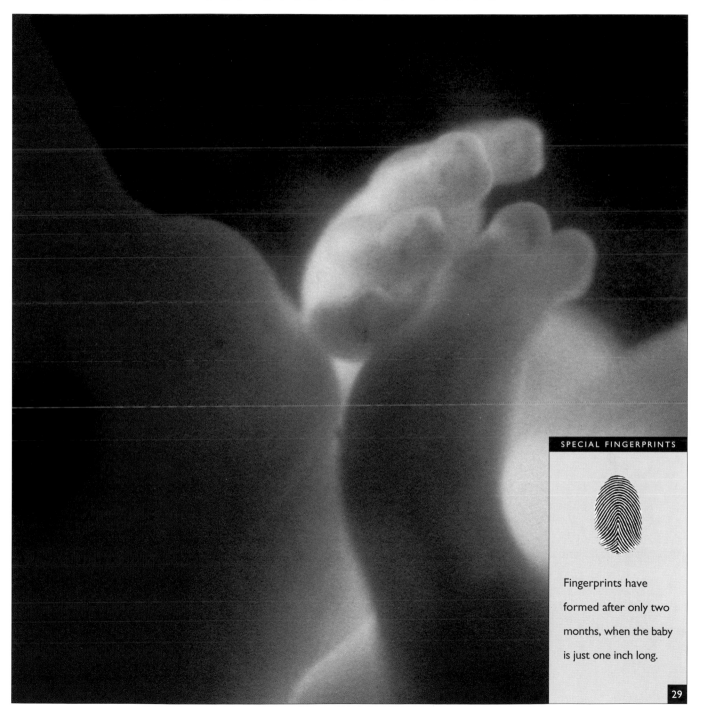

SPECIAL FINGERPRINTS

Fingerprints have formed after only two months, when the baby is just one inch long.

29

W*hat did I look like?*

You looked a lot like this. Weren't you cute?

Ohhh! Did I live in a balloon like that?

It does look like a balloon, doesn't it? That's the little bubble

where you lived. Inside it was watery and warm.

FOUR MONTHS OLD

Inside the amniotic sac, the baby can now make facial expressions, as well as move fingers and toes.

31

What did I do in there?

Sometimes you sucked your thumb. Sometimes you
waved your arms. Sometimes I felt a kick from your little feet.
All that exercise made you tired, so you slept a lot, too.
Sometimes I sang lullabies.
Even from inside, you could hear my voice.

TWENTY WEEKS OLD

Now the mother can first begin feeling the kicks and movements of the baby inside her.

33

What *did I eat?*

Lots of good things. You ate everything I ate.

How?

Do you know where your
bellybutton is?

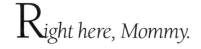

Well, when you were inside me,
all your food came from me to you through a tube called
the umbilical cord. It went right inside you,
where your belly button is now.

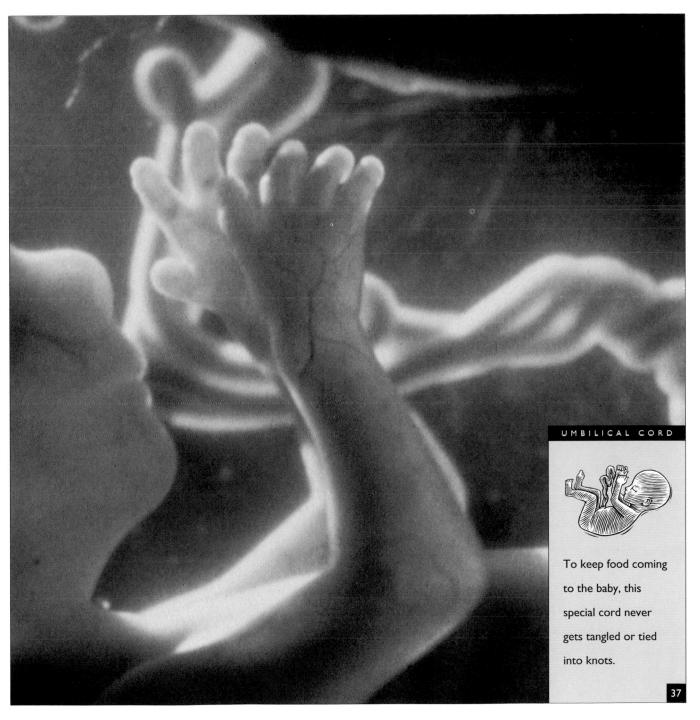

UMBILICAL CORD

To keep food coming to the baby, this special cord never gets tangled or tied into knots.

37

With all that good food,
you grew and grew and grew.
After about nine months you were too big
to stay inside Mommy anymore.
It was time to come out.

When God was ready for you to be born,
you left the uterus and came outside through
a little tunnel called a birth canal.
First we saw your head.
Then your whole body came out.

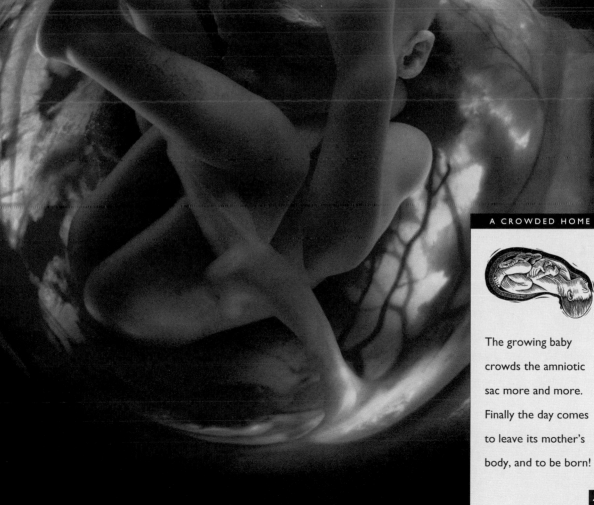

A CROWDED HOME

The growing baby crowds the amniotic sac more and more. Finally the day comes to leave its mother's body, and to be born!

41

We were so happy to see you.
We thanked God for making such a beautiful baby,
and now He is making you into
a fine young person.

Mommy, I like how God made me!

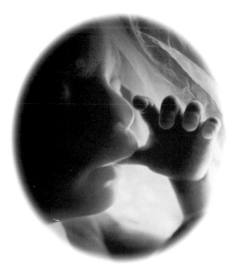

You made all the delicate,
inner parts of my body and knit them together
in my mother's womb.

PSALM 139:13 (THE LIVING BIBLE)